PUBLIC LIBRARY, DISTRICT OF COLUMBIA

D0998460

George H. W. Bush

BY MIRELLA S. MILLER

Published by The Child's World®
1980 Lookout Drive • Mankato, MN 56003-1705
800-599-READ • www.childsworld.com

Photographs ©: Library of Congress, cover, 1; White House/
CNP/ABACAUSA.COM/Newscom, 4; Bridgeman Images, 7;
Everett Collection/Newscom, 8; AP Images, 11; Unimedia
International/Newscom, 12; Barry Soorenko - CNP/
Newscom, 15; Ron Edmonds/AP Images, 16; Barry Thumma/
AP Images, 19; Gabriel Chmielewski/College Station Eagle/
AP Images, 20

Copyright © 2017 by The Child's World®
All rights reserved. No part of this book may be reproduced
or utilized in any form or by any means without written
permission from the publisher.

ISBN 9781503816459
LCCN 2016945614

Printed in the United States of America
PAO2322

ABOUT THE AUTHOR

Mirella S. Miller is an author and editor of several children's books. She lives in Minnesota with her husband and their dog.

Table of Contents

★ ★ ★

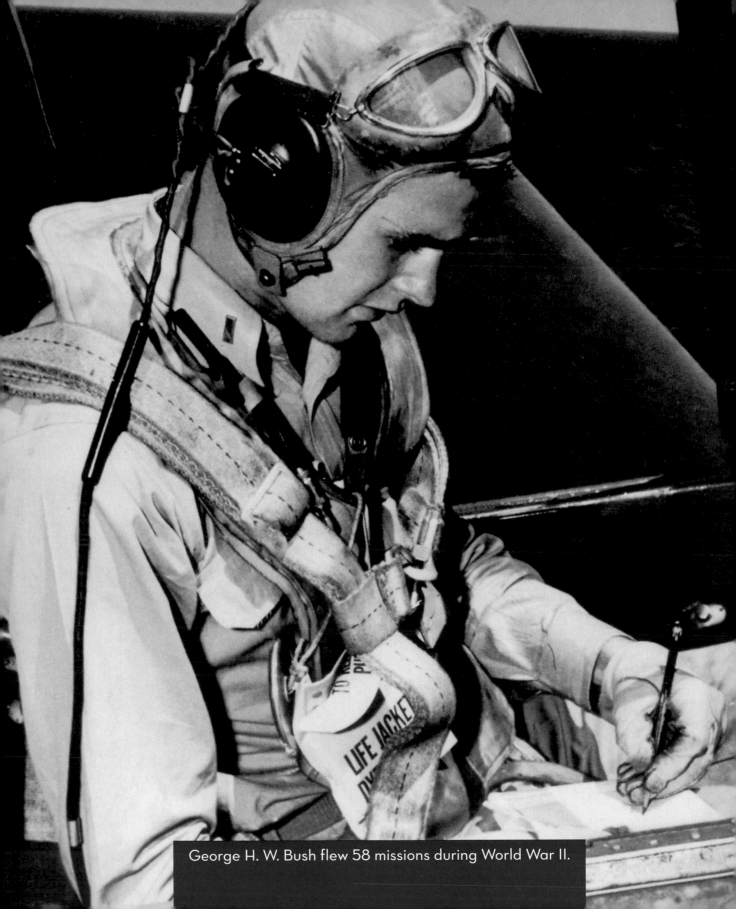

George H. W. Bush flew 58 missions during World War II.

CHAPTER ONE

Rescued in the Pacific Ocean

It was 1944. The United States was fighting in World War II. Japan had bombed Pearl Harbor in December 1941. That is a military base in Hawaii. After the attack, people signed up to fight. One of those people was George H. W. Bush. He joined the U.S. Navy. He was 18 years old.

Bush was a pilot. He flew planes that attacked ships by dropping bombs. Bush went on many successful jobs. But one ended differently.

It was September 2, 1944. Bush was sent to attack an enemy site. Other pilots went, too. The site was on an island near Japan. As Bush got closer, there was gunfire. Bush and the other pilots were under attack.

The engine on Bush's plane was hit. It caught fire. He was going to crash. Bush released the bombs from his plane. Then he turned his plane around. He had no time to get to safety. Bush had to jump out of the plane. He landed in the Pacific Ocean.

Bush found something to float on. He didn't know how long he would be waiting. He hoped U.S. troops would save him soon. A U.S. submarine crew found him four hours later. Bush received a medal for his brave actions. His bravery would also help him later in life. He would make big decisions one day as president.

Bush (center) on the aircraft carrier USS *San Jacinto*

Bush is the second oldest in his family.

CHAPTER TWO

Bush's Early Life

George Herbert Walker Bush was born on June 12, 1924. He was born in Milton, Massachusetts. George was one of five children. The family moved to Connecticut when George was young. His father, Prescott, was a state senator. The Bushes were rich. But they taught George to give back to others.

George went to **boarding school** in Andover, Massachusetts. He played baseball and soccer at school. He was also the senior class president. George finished high school in 1942.

He joined the U.S. Navy that year. George became a pilot in 1943. He was the youngest pilot in the navy.

On January 6, 1945, George married Barbara Pierce. They met three years earlier at a dance. Their first son, George Walker, was born in 1946. They went on to have five more kids. Their names are Robin, Jeb, Neil, Marvin, and Dorothy.

George and Barbara moved to Connecticut in 1945. George started college at Yale University. He finished quickly and graduated in 1948. George moved his young family to Texas. He began working for an oil company. George bought and sold land. He also started new companies. George did well in the oil business. He made a lot of money. George wanted to follow in his father's footsteps. He decided to go into **politics**.

Bush earned a degree in economics at Yale University.

Bush was the first vice president to be elected president since 1836.

CHAPTER FOUR

Becoming President

In 1989, many things were changing around the world. The Cold War was ending. The Berlin Wall fell. It seemed the world might be more peaceful.

This changed on August 2, 1990. Iraq attacked Kuwait. Their leader wanted Kuwait's oil. Bush knew this needed to stop. He sent troops overseas. Bush had help from 32 other countries. Together they stopped Iraq.

Bush also had successes back home. He signed important acts into law in 1990.

The first was the Americans with Disabilities Act. It helped people with disabilities be treated as equals. Bush also signed the Clean Air Act. This lowered the amount of air **pollution**.

Helping the community was important to Bush. He felt more Americans should help others. He signed the National and Community Service Act. This act created more service groups around the country.

Bush was a popular president. He had many successes. But there were issues while he was president. The **economy** and city crime were problems. Bush ran for president again in 1992. But he lost to Bill Clinton.

Bush left the White House. He moved back to Texas. Bush continued helping **charities**. He raised millions of dollars. He helped hospitals. He also worked with churches.

Bush worked with many people to increase community service groups across the country.

Bush has been skydiving eight times.

Bush helped plan his presidential library, too. It opened in 1997. It is in College Station, Texas.

Bush's sons also work in politics. George W. was governor of Texas. Then he became president in 2001. Bush is only the second president to have a son become president. Jeb served as governor of Florida. He also wanted to become president. In 2016, Jeb tried. He ran to be the Republican presidential candidate. But he did not win.

Bush enjoys golfing and playing tennis. He also likes jumping out of airplanes. He celebrated his 90th birthday with a jump. Bush has homes in Texas and Maine. He likes spending time with his family. He even works with other presidents to help people.

TIMELINE

1920

← **June 12, 1924** George Herbert Walker Bush is born in Milton, Massachusetts.

← **June 12, 1942** Bush graduates from high school and joins the U.S. Navy.

← **September 2, 1944** Bush is shot down by the Japanese during WWII and rescued by a U.S. submarine.

← **January 6, 1945** Bush marries Barbara Pierce.

← **July 6, 1946** George Walker Bush is born.

← **Summer 1948** The Bushes move to Texas. Bush begins working in the oil industry.

← **February 11, 1953** John Ellis "Jeb" Bush is born.

← **1962** Bush becomes chairman of the Republican Party in Harris County, Texas.

← **1966** Bush is elected to the U.S. House of Representatives.

← **December 11, 1970** President Richard Nixon makes Bush the U.S. ambassador to the United Nations.

← **January 20, 1981** Bush is sworn in as the 43rd vice president of the United States.

← **January 20, 1989** Bush is sworn in as the 41st president of the United States.

← **January 1992** Bush leaves office.

1995

ambassador (am-BASS-uh-dur) An ambassador is the highest-ranking person who represents his or her government in another country. Bush was the U.S. ambassador to the United Nations.

boarding school (BORD-ing SKOOL) A boarding school is a school where students also live. Bush attended boarding school in Massachusetts.

chairman (CHAYR-muhn) A chairman is a person who is in charge of a committee or a group. Bush served as the RNC chairman.

charities (CHAYR-i-tees) Charities are groups that help people in need. Bush helped raise money for many charities.

Congress (KONG-griss) The U.S. Congress includes the Senate and the House of Representatives. Bush served in Congress for two terms.

economy (i-KON-uh-me) The economy is a system through which goods and services are sold and bought. There were problems with the economy during Bush's presidency.

politics (POL-uh-tiks) Politics are activities to gain or hold onto power in government. Bush worked in politics.

pollution (puh-LOO-shuhn) Pollution is when dirty substances are released into the environment. Bush's Clean Air Act helped clean up pollution.

popular (POP-yuh-lur) To be popular means to be liked by many people. Bush was a popular president.

Republican Party (ri-PUHB-li-kuhn PAR-tee) The Republican Party is a major political party in the United States. Bush was a member of the Republican Party.

In the Library

Francis, Sandra. *George Bush*. Mankato, MN: The Child's World, 2009.

Shea, Therese. *Famous Texans*. New York: PowerKids Press, 2014.

Venezia, Mike. *George Bush: Forty-First President, 1989–1993*. New York: Children's Press, 2008.

On the Web

Visit our Web site for links about George H. W. Bush:
childsworld.com/links

Note to Parents, Teachers, and Librarians: We routinely verify our Web links to make sure they are safe and active sites. So encourage your readers to check them out!

INDEX